APRIL TWILIGHTS
AND OTHER POEMS

APRIL TWILIGHTS

AND OTHER POEMS

BY

WILLA CATHER

ALFRED A KNOPF
NEW YORK · MCMXXXIII

Published, April, 1923
Second Printing, January, 1924
Third Printing, January, 1933
Fourth Printing, June, 1933

MANUFACTURED IN THE UNITED STATES OF AMERICA

To my Father
for a Valentine

THE verses in Part I of this volume are reprinted from an early volume, APRIL TWILIGHTS, published in 1903. Those in Part II are of later composition, and for permission to republish them I am indebted to the editors of SCRIBNER'S MAGAZINE, McCLURE'S MAGAZINE, and the CENTURY MAGAZINE.

WILLA CATHER

CONTENTS

PART I

APRIL TWILIGHTS

AND OTHER POEMS

࿎

"GRANDMITHER, THINK NOT I FORGET"

Grandmither, think not I forget, when I come back to town,
An' wander the old ways again an' tread them up an' down.
I never smell the clover bloom, nor see the swallows pass,
Without I mind how good ye were unto a little lass.
I never hear the winter rain a-pelting all night through,
Without I think and mind me of how cold it falls on you.
And if I come not often to your bed beneath the thyme,
Mayhap 't is that I'd change wi' ye, and gie my bed for thine,
  Would like to sleep in thine.

I never hear the summer winds among the roses blow,
Without I wonder why it was ye loved the lassie so.
Ye gave me cakes and lollipops and pretty toys a score,—
I never thought I should come back and ask ye now for more.
Grandmither, gie me your still, white hands, that lie upon your breast,
For mine do beat the dark all night and never find me rest;
They grope among the shadows an' they beat the cold black air,
They go seekin' in the darkness, an' they never find him there,
  An' they never find him there.

Grandmither, gie me your sightless eyes, that I may never see
His own a-burnin' full o' love that must not shine for me.
Grandmither, gie me your peaceful lips, white as the kirkyard snow,
For mine be red wi' burnin' thirst, an' he must never know.
Grandmither, gie me your clay-stopped ears, that I may never hear
My lad a-singin' in the night when I am sick wi' fear;
A-singin' when the moonlight over a' the land is white—
Aw God! I'll up an' go to him a-singin' in the night,
        A-callin' in the night.

Grandmither, gie me your clay-cold heart that has forgot to ache,
For mine be fire within my breast and yet it cannot break.
It beats an' throbs forever for the things that must not be,—
An' can ye not let me creep in an' rest awhile by ye?
A little lass afeard o' dark slept by ye years agone—
Ah, she has found what night can hold 'twixt sunset an' the dawn!
So when I plant the rose an' rue above your grave for ye,
Ye'll know it's under rue an' rose that I would like to be,
        That I would like to be.

FIDES, SPES

Joy is come to the little
    Everywhere;
Pink to the peach and pink to the apple,
    White to the pear.
Stars are come to the dogwood,
    Astral, pale;
Mists are pink on the red-bud,
    Veil after veil.
Flutes for the feathery locusts,
    Soft as spray;
Tongues of lovers for chestnuts, poplars,
    Babbling May.
Yellow plumes for the willows'
    Wind-blown hair;
Oak trees and sycamores only
    Comfortless, bare.
Sore from steel and the watching,
    Somber and old,
(Wooing robes for the beeches, larches,
    Splashed with gold,
Breath of love from the lilacs,
    Warm with noon,)
Great hearts cold when the little
    Beat mad so soon.
What is their faith to bear it
    Till it come,
Waiting with rain-cloud and swallow,
    Frozen, dumb?

THE TAVERN

In the tavern of my heart
    Many a one has sat before,
Drunk red wine and sung a stave,
    And, departing, come no more.
When the night was cold without,
    And the ravens croaked of storm,
They have sat them at my hearth,
    Telling me my house was warm.

As the lute and cup went round,
    They have rhymed me well in lay;—
When the hunt was on at morn,
    Each, departing, went his way.
On the walls, in compliment,
    Some would scrawl a verse or two,
Some have hung a willow branch,
    Or a wreath of corn-flowers blue.

Ah! my friend, when thou dost go,
    Leave no wreath of flowers for me;
Not pale daffodils nor rue,
    Violets nor rosemary.
Spill the wine upon the lamps,
    Tread the fire, and bar the door;
So despoil the wretched place,
    None will come forevermore.

THE HAWTHORN TREE

Across the shimmering meadows—
Ah, when he came to me!
In the spring-time,
In the night-time,
In the starlight,
Beneath the hawthorn tree.

Up from the misty marsh-land—
Ah, when he climbed to me!
To my white bower,
To my sweet rest,
To my warm breast,
Beneath the hawthorn tree.

Ask of me what the birds sang,
High in the hawthorn tree;
What the breeze tells,
What the rose smells,
What the stars shine—
Not what he said to me!

Does the darkness cradle thee
Than mine arms more tenderly?
Do the angels God hath put
    There to guard thy lonely sleep—
One at head and one at foot—
    Watch more fond and constant keep?
When the black-bird sings in May,
    And the spring is in the wood,
Would you never trudge the way
    Over hill-tops, if you could?
Was my harp so hard a load
    Even on the sunny morns
When the plumèd huntsmen rode
    To the music of their horns?
Hath the love that lit the stars,
    Fills the sea and moulds the flowers,
Whose completeness nothing mars,
    Made forgot what once was ours?
Christ hath perfect rest to give—
    Stillness and perpetual peace;
You, who found it hard to live,
    Sleep and sleep, without surcease.

Christ hath stars to light thy porch,
    Silence after fevered song;—
I had but a minstrel's torch
    And the way was wet and long.

[18]

Sleep. No more on winter nights,
    Harping at some castle gate,
Thou must see the revel lights
    Stream upon our cold estate.
Bitter was the bread of song
    While you tarried in my tent,
And the jeering of the throng
    Hurt you, as it came and went.
When you slept upon my breast
    Grief had wed me long ago:
Christ hath his perpetual rest
    For thy weariness. But oh!
When I sleep beside the road,
    Thanking God thou liest not so,
Brother to the owl and toad,
    Could'st thou, Dear, but let me know,
Does the darkness cradle thee
Than mine arms more tenderly?

With attributes of gods they sculptured him,
　　Hermes, Osiris, but were never wise
To lift the level, frowning brow of him
　　Or dull the mortal misery in his eyes,
The scornful weariness of every limb,
　　The dust-begotten doubt that never dies,
Antinous, beneath thy lids, though dim,
The curling smoke of altars rose to thee,
Conjuring thee to comfort and content.
　　An emperor sent his galleys wide and far
To seek thy healing for thee. Yea, and spent
　　Honour and treasure and red fruits of war
　　To lift thy heaviness, lest thou should'st mar
The head that was an empire's glory, bent
A little, as the heavy poppies are.
　　Did the perfection of thy beauty pain
Thy limbs to bear it? Did it ache to be,
　　As song hath ached in men, or passion vain?
Or lay it like some heavy robe on thee?
　　Was thy sick soul drawn from thee like the rain,
Or drunk up as the dead are drunk each hour
To feed the colour of some tulip flower?

LONDON ROSES

"Rowses, Rowses! Penny a bunch!" they tell you—
Slattern girls in Trafalgar, eager to sell you.
Roses, roses, red in the Kensington sun,
Holland Road, High Street, Bayswater, see you and smell you—
Roses of London town, red till the summer is done.

Roses, roses, locust and lilac, perfuming
West End, East End, wondrously budding and blooming
Out of the black earth, rubbed in a million hands,
Foot-trod, sweat-sour over and under, entombing
Highways of darkness, deep gutted with iron bands.

"Rowses, rowses! Penny a bunch!" they tell you,
Ruddy blooms of corruption, see you and smell you,
Born of stale earth, fallowed with squalor and tears—
North shire, south shire, none are like these, I tell you,
Roses of London perfumed with a thousand years.

Cold are the stars of the night,
　Wild is the tempest crying,
Fast through the velvet dark
　Little white flakes are flying.
Still is the House of Song.
　　But the fire on the hearth is burning;
And the lamps are trimmed, and the cup
　Is full for his day of returning.
His watchers are fallen asleep,
　They wait but his call to follow,
Ay, to the ends of the earth—
　But Apollo, the god, Apollo?

Sick is the heart in my breast,
　Mine eyes are blinded with weeping;
The god who never comes back,
　The watch that forever is keeping.
Service of gods is hard;
　Deep lies the snow on my pillow.
For him the laurel and song,
　Weeping for me and the willow:
Empty my arms and cold
　As the nest forgot of the swallow;
Birds will come back with the spring,—
　But Apollo, the god, Apollo?

Hope will come back with the spring,
  Joy with the lark's returning;
Love must awake betimes,
  When crocus buds are a-burning.
Hawthorns will follow the snow,
  The robin his tryst be keeping;
Winds will blow in the May,
  Waking the pulses a-sleeping.
Snowdrops will whiten the hills,
  Violets hide in the hollow:
Pan will be drunken and rage—
  But Apollo, the god, Apollo?

PARADOX

I knew them both upon Miranda's isle,
    Which is of youth a sea-bound seigniory:
Misshapen Caliban, so seeming vile,
    And Ariel, proud prince of minstrelsy,
Who did forsake the sunset for my tower
    And like a star above my slumber burned.
The night was held in silver chains by power
    Of melody, in which all longings yearned—
Star-grasping youth in one wild strain expressed,
    Tender as dawn, insistent as the tide;
The heart of night and summer stood confessed.
    I rose aglow and flung the lattice wide—
Ah, jest of art, what mockery and pang!
    Alack, it was poor Caliban who sang.

IN MEDIA VITA

Streams of the spring a-singing,
    Winds of the May that blow,
Birds from the Southland winging,
    Buds in the grasses below.
Clouds that speed hurrying over,
    And the climbing rose by the wall,
Singing of bees in the clover,
    And the dead, under all!

Lads and their sweethearts lying
    In the cleft of the windy hill;
Hearts that are hushed of their sighing,
    Lips that are tender and still.
Stars in the purple gloaming,
    Flowers that suffuse and fall,
Twitter of bird-mates homing,
    And the dead, under all!

Herdsman abroad with his collie,
    Girls on their way to the fair,
Young lads a-chasing their folly,
    Parsons a-praying their prayer.
Children their kites a-flying,
    Grandsires that nod by the wall,
Mothers soft lullabies sighing,
    And the dead, under all!

EVENING SONG

Dear love, what thing of all the things that be
Is ever worth one thought from you or me,
    Save only Love,
    Save only Love?

The days so short, the nights so quick to flee,
The world so wide, so deep and dark the sea,
    So dark the sea;

So far the suns and every listless star,
Beyond their light—Ah! dear, who knows how far,
    Who knows how far?

One thing of all dim things I know is true,
The heart within me knows, and tells it you,
    And tells it you.

So blind is life, so long at last is sleep,
And none but Love to bid us laugh or weep,
    And none but Love,
    And none but Love.

LAMENT FOR MARSYAS

Marsyas sleeps. Oh, never wait,
Maidens, by the city gate,
Till he come to plunder gold
Of the daffodils you hold,
Or your branches white with may;
He is whiter gone than they.
He will startle you no more
When along the river shore
Damsels beat the linen clean.
Nor when maidens play at ball
Will he catch it where it fall:
Though ye wait for him and call,
He will answer not, I ween.

Happy Earth to hold him so,
Still and satisfied and low,
Giving him his will—ah, more
Than a woman could before!
Still forever holding up
To his parted lips the cup
Which hath eased him, when to bless
All who loved were powerless.
Ah! for that too-lovely head,
Low among the laureled dead,
Many a rose earth oweth yet;
Many a yellow jonquil brim,
Many a hyacinth dewy-dim,
For the singing breath of him—
Sweeter than the violet.

I sought the wood in summer
    When every twig was green;
The rudest boughs were tender,
    And buds were pink between.
Light-fingered aspens trembled
    In fitful sun and shade,
And daffodils were golden
    In every starry glade.
The brook sang like a robin—
    My hand could check him where
The lissome maiden willows
    Shook out their yellow hair.

"How frail a thing is Beauty,"
    I said, "when every breath
She gives the vagrant summer
    But swifter woos her death.
For this the star dust troubles,
    For this have ages rolled:
To deck the wood for bridal
    And slay her with the cold."

I sought the wood in winter
    When every leaf was dead;
Behind the wind-whipped branches
    The winter sun set red.
The coldest star was rising
    To greet that bitter air,

The oaks were writhen giants;
    Nor bud nor bloom was there.
The birches, white and slender,
    In deathless marble stood,
The brook, a white immortal,
    Slept silent in the wood.

"How sure a thing is Beauty,"
    I cried. "No bolt can slay,
No wave nor shock despoil her,
    No ravishers dismay.
Her warriors are the angels
    That cherish from afar,
Her warders people Heaven
    And watch from every star.
The granite hills are slighter,
    The sea more like to fail;
Behind the rose the planet,
    The Law behind the veil."

Sleep, minstrel, sleep; the winter wind's awake,
    And yellow April's buried deep and cold.
The wood is black, and songful things forsake
    The haunted forest when the year is old.
Above the drifted snow the aspens quake,
    The scourging clouds a shrunken moon enfold,
Denying all that nights of summer spake
    And swearing false the summer's globe of gold.

Sleep, minstrel, sleep; in such a bitter night
    Thine azure song would seek the stars in vain;
Thy rose and roundelay the winter's spite
    Would scarcely spare—O never wake again!
These leaden skies do not thy masques invite,
    Thy sunny breath would warm not their disdain;
How should'st thou sing to boughs with winter dight,
    Or gather marigolds in winter rain?

Sleep, minstrel, sleep; we do not grow more kind;
    Your cloak was thin, your wound was wet and deep;
More bitter breath there was than winter wind,
    And hotter tears than now thy lovers weep.
Upon the world-old breast of comfort find
    How gentle Darkness thee will gently keep.
Thou wert the summer's, and thy joy declined
    When winter winds awoke. Sleep, minstrel, sleep.

IN ROSE-TIME

Oh, this is the joy of the rose:
That it blows,
And goes.

Winter lasts a five-month,
    Spring-time stays but one;
Yellow blow the rye-fields
    When the rose is done.
Pines are clad at Yuletide
    When the birch is bare,
And the holly's greenest
    In the frosty air.

Sorrow keeps a stone house
    Builded grim and gray;
Pleasure hath a straw thatch
    Hung with lanterns gay.
On her petty savings
    Niggard Prudence thrives,
Passion, ere the moonset,
    Bleeds a thousand lives.

Virtue hath a warm hearth—
    Folly's dead and drowned;
Friendship hath her own when
    Love is underground.
Ah! for me the madness
    Of the spendthrift flower,
Burning myriad sunsets
    In a single hour.

For this is the joy of the rose:
    That it blows,
        And goes.

POPPIES ON LUDLOW CASTLE

Through halls of vanished pleasure,
     And hold of vanished power,
And crypt of faith forgotten,
     I came to Ludlow tower.

A-top of arch and stairway,
     Of crypt, and donjon cell,
Of council hall, and chamber,
     Of wall, and ditch, and well,

High over grated turrets
     Where clinging ivies run,
A thousand scarlet poppies
     Enticed the rising sun,

Upon the topmost turret,
     With death and damp below,—
Three hundred years of spoilage,—
     The crimson poppies grow.

This hall it was that bred him,
     These hills that knew him brave,
The gentlest English singer
     That fills an English grave.

How have they heart to blossom
    So cruel gay and red,
When beauty so hath perished
    And valour so hath sped?

When knights so fair are rotten,
    And captains true asleep,
And singing lips are dust-stopped
    Six English earth-feet deep?

When ages old remind me
    How much hath gone for naught,
What wretched ghost remaineth
    Of all that flesh hath wrought;

Of love and song and warring,
    Of adventure and play,
Of art and comely building,
    Of faith and form and fray—

I'll mind the flowers of pleasure,
    Of short-lived youth and sleep,
That drank the sunny weather
    A-top of Ludlow keep.

PRAIRIE DAWN

A crimson fire that vanquishes the stars;
A pungent odor from the dusty sage;
A sudden stirring of the huddled herds;
A breaking of the distant table-lands
Through purple mists ascending, and the flare
Of water-ditches silver in the light;
A swift, bright lance hurled low across the world;
A sudden sickness for the hills of home.

AFTERMATH

Canst thou conjure a vanished morn of spring,
     Or bid the ashes of the sunset glow
Again to redness? Are we strong to wring
     From trodden grapes the juice drunk long ago?
Can leafy longings stir in autumn's blood,
     Or can I wear a pearl dissolved in wine,
Or go a-Maying in a winter wood,
     Or paint with youth thy wasted cheek, or mine?
What bloom, then, shall abide, since ours hath sped?
     Thou art more lost to me than they who dwell
In Egypt's sepulchres, long ages fled;
     And would I touch—Ah me! I might as well
Covet the gold of Helen's vanished head,
     Or kiss back Cleopatra from the dead!

THOU ART THE PEARL

I read of knights who laid their armour down,
    And left the tourney's prize for other hands,
And clad them in a pilgrim's sober gown,
    To seek a holy cup in desert lands.
For them no more the torch of victory;
    For them lone vigils and the starlight pale,
So they in dreams the Blessed Cup may see—
    Thou art the Grail!

An Eastern king once smelled a rose in sleep,
    And on the morrow laid his scepter down.
His heir his titles and his lands might keep,—
    The rose was sweeter wearing than the crown.
Nor cared he that its life was but an hour,
    A breath that from the crimson summer blows,
Who gladly paid a kingdom for a flower—
    Thou art the Rose!

A merchant man, who knew the worth of things,
    Beheld a pearl more priceless than a star;
And straight returning, all he hath he brings
    And goes upon his way, ah, richer far!
Laughter of merchants in the market-place,
    Nor taunting gibe nor scornful lips that curl,
Can ever cloud the rapture on his face—
    Thou art the Pearl!

ARCADIAN WINTER

Woe is me to tell it thee,
Winter winds in Arcady!
Scattered is thy flock and fled
From the glades where once it fed,
And the snow lies drifted white
In the bower of our delight,
Where the beech threw gracious shade
On the cheek of boy and maid:
And the bitter blasts make roar
Through the fleshless sycamore.

White enchantment holds the spring,
Where thou once wert wont to sing,
And the cold hath cut to death
Reeds melodious of thy breath.
He, the rival of thy lyre,
Nightingale with note of fire,
Sings no more; but far away,
From the windy hill-side gray,
Calls the broken note forlorn
Of an aged shepherd's horn.

Still about the fire they tell
How it long ago befell
That a shepherd maid and lad
Met and trembled and were glad;
When the swift spring waters ran,

And the wind to boy or man
Brought the aching of his sires—
Song and love and all desires.
Ere the starry dogwoods fell
They were lovers, so they tell.

Woe is me to tell it thee,
Winter winds in Arcady!
Broken pipes and vows forgot,
Scattered flocks returning not,
Frozen brook and drifted hill,
Ashen sun and song-birds still;
Songs of summer and desire
Crooned about the winter fire;
Shepherd lads with silver hair,
Shepherd maids no longer fair.

PROVENÇAL LEGEND

On his little grave and wild,
Faustinus, the martyr child,
 Candytuft and mustards grow.
Ah, how many a June has smiled
 On the turf he lies below.

Ages gone they laid him there,
Quit of sun and wholesome air,
 Broken flesh and tortured limb;
Leaving all his faith the heir
 Of his gentle hope and him.

Yonder, under pagan skies,
Bleached by rains, the circus lies,
 Where they brought him from his play.
Comeliest his of sacrifice,
 Youth and tender April day.

"Art thou not the shepherd's son?—
There the hills thy lambkins run?—
 These the fields thy brethren keep?"
"On a higher hill than yon
 Doth my Father lead His sheep."

"Bring thy ransom, then," they say,
"Gold enough to pave the way
 From the temple to the Rhone."
When he came, upon his day,
 Slender, tremulous, alone,

Mustard flowers like these he pressed,
Golden, flame-like, to his breast,
   Blooms the early weanlings eat.
When his Triumph brought him rest,
   Yellow bloom lay at his feet.

Golden play-days came: the air
Called him, weanlings bleated there,
   Roman boys ran fleet with spring;
Shorn of youth and usage fair,
   Hope nor hill-top days they bring.

But the shepherd children still
Come at Easter, warm or chill,
   Come with violets gathered wild
From his sloping pasture hill,
Play-fellows who would fulfill
   Play-time to that martyr child.

THE ENCORE

No garlands in the winter-time,
    No trumpets in the night!
The song ye praise was done lang syne,
    And was its own delight.
O' God's name take the wreath away,
    Since now the music's sped;
Ye never cry, "Long live the king!"
    Until the king is dead.

When I came piping through the land,
    One morning in the spring,
With cockle-burrs upon my coat,
    'Twas then I was a king:
A mullein sceptre in my hand,
    My order daisies three,
With song's first freshness on my lips—
    And then ye pitied me!

SONG

Troubadour, when you were gay,
You wooed with rose and roundelay,
Singing harp-strings, sweet as May.
From beneath the crown of bay
Fell the wild, abundant hair.
Scent of cherry bloom and pear
With you from the south did fare,
Buds of myrtle for your wear.
Soft as summer stars thine eyes,
Planets pale in violet skies;
Summer wind that sings and dies
Was the music of thy sighs.

Troubadour, one winter's night,
When the pasture-lands were white
And the cruel stars were bright,
Fortune held thee in despite.
Then beneath my tower you bore
Rose nor rondel as of yore,
But a heavy grief and sore
Laid in silence at my door.
April yearneth, April goes;
Not for me her violet blows,
I have done for long with those.
At my breast thy sorrow grows,
Nearer to my heart, God knows,
Than ever roundelay or rose!

L'ENVOI

Where are the loves that we have loved before
When once we are alone, and shut the door?
No matter whose the arms that held me fast,
The arms of Darkness hold me at the last.
No matter down what primrose path I tend,
I kiss the lips of Silence in the end.
No matter on what heart I found delight,
I come again unto the breast of Night.
No matter when or how love did befall,
'Tis Loneliness that loves me best of all,
And in the end she claims me, and I know
That she will stay, though all the rest may go.
No matter whose the eyes that I would keep
Near in the dark, 'tis in the eyes of Sleep
That I must look and look forever more,
When once I am alone, and shut the door.

PART II

THE PALATINE

"Have you been with the King to Rome,
  Brother, big brother?"
"I've been there and I've come home.
  Back to your play, little brother."

"Oh, how high is Caesar's house,
  Brother, big brother?"
"Goats about the doorways browse:
Night hawks nest in the burnt roof-tree,
Home of the wild bird and home of the bee.
A thousand chambers of marble lie
Wide to the sun and the wind and the sky.
Poppies we find amongst our wheat
Grow on Caesar's banquet seat.
Cattle crop and neatherds drowse
On the floors of Caesar's house."

"But what has become of Caesar's gold,
  Brother, big brother?"
"The times are bad and the world is old—
Who knows the where of the Caesars' gold?
Night comes black on the Caesars' hill;
The wells are deep and the tales are ill.
Fire-flies gleam in the damp and mould,—
All that is left of the Caesars' gold.
  Back to your play, little brother."

"What has become of the Caesars' men,
  Brother, big brother?"
"Dogs in the kennel and wolf in the den
Howl for the fate of the Caesars' men.
Slain in Asia, slain in Gaul,
By Dacian border and Persian wall;
Rhineland orchard and Danube fen
Fatten their roots on Caesar's men."

"Why is the world so sad and wide,
  Brother, big brother?"
"Saxon boys by their fields that bide
Need not know if the world is wide.
Climb no mountain but Shire-end Hill,
Cross no water but goes to mill;
Ox in the stable and cow in the byre,
Smell of the wood smoke and sleep by the fire;
Sun-up in seed-time—a likely lad
Hurts not his head that the world is sad.
  Back to your play, little brother."

The murmur of old, old water,
    The yellow of old, old stone,
The fountain that sings through the silence,
    The river-god, dreaming alone;
The Antonine booted and mounted
    In his sun-lit, hill-top place,
The Julians, gigantic in armour,
    The low-browed Claudian race.

The wolf and the twin boys she suckled,
    And the powerful breed they bred;
Caesars of duplicate empires,
    All under one roof-stead.
Fronting these fronts triumphant,
    Conquest on conquest pressed
By these marching, arrogant masters,
    Who could have hoped for the West?

At the feet of his multiple victors,
    Beaten and dazed and dumb,
One, from the wild new races,
    Clay of the kings to come.
Hail, in the halls of the Caesars!
    Hail, from the thrones oversea!
Sheath of the sword-like vigour,
    Sap of the kings to be!

A LIKENESS
(PORTRAIT BUST OF AN UNKNOWN, CAPITOL, ROME)

In every line a supple beauty—
  The restless head a little bent—
Disgust of pleasure, scorn of duty,
  The unseeing eyes of discontent.
I often come to sit beside him,
  This youth who passed and left no trace
Of good or ill that did betide him,
  Save the disdain upon his face.

The hope of all his House, the brother
  Adored, the golden-hearted son,
Whom Fortune pampered like a mother;
  And then—a shadow on the sun.
Whether he followed Caesar's trumpet,
  Or chanced the riskier game at home
To find how favour played the strumpet
  In fickle politics at Rome;

Whether he dreamed a dream in Asia
  He never could forget by day,
Or gave his youth to some Aspasia,
  Or gamed his heritage away—
Once lost, across the Empire's border
  This man would seek his peace in vain;
His look arraigns a social order
  Somehow entrammelled with his pain.

"The dice of gods are always loaded";
  One gambler, arrogant as they,
Fierce, and by fierce injustice goaded,
  Left both his hazard and the play.
Incapable of compromises,
  Unable to forgive or spare,
The strange awarding of the prizes
  He had no fortitude to bear.

Tricked by the forms of things material,—
  The solid-seeming arch and stone,
The noise of war, the pomp Imperial,
  The heights and depths about a throne—
He missed, among the shapes diurnal,
  The old, deep-travelled road from pain,
The thoughts of men, which are eternal,
  In which, eternal, men remain.

Ritratto d'ignoto; defying
  Things unsubstantial as a dream—
An empire, long in ashes lying—
  His face still set against the stream—
Yes, so he looked, that gifted brother
  I loved, who passed and left no trace,
Not even—luckier than this other—
  His sorrow in a marble face.

THE SWEDISH MOTHER
(NEBRASKA)

"You shall hear the tale again—
Hush, my red-haired daughter."
Brightly burned the sunset gold
On the black pond water.

Red the pasture ridges gleamed
Where the sun was sinking.
Slow the windmill rasped and wheezed
Where the herd was drinking.

On the kitchen doorstep low
Sat a Swedish mother;
In her arms one baby slept,
By her sat another.

"All time, 'way back in old countree,
Your grandpa, he been good to me.
Your grandpa, he been young man, too,
And I been yust li'l' girl, like you.
All time in spring, when evening come,
We go bring sheep an' li'l' lambs home.
We go big field, 'way up on hill,
Ten times high like our windmill.
One time your grandpa leave me wait
While he call sheep down. By de gate
I sit still till night come dark;
Rabbits run an' strange dogs bark,
Old owl hoot, an' your modder cry,
She been so 'fraid big bear come by.

Last, 'way off, she hear de sheep,
Li'l' bells ring and li'l' lambs bleat.
Then all sheep come over de hills,
Big white dust, an' old dog Nils.
Then come grandpa, in his arm
Li'l' sick lamb dat somet'ing harm.
He so young then, big and strong,
Pick li'l' girl up, take her 'long,—
Poor li'l' tired girl, yust like you,—
Lift her up an' take her too.
Hold her tight an' carry her far,—
Ain't no light but yust one star.
Sheep go 'bah-h,' an' road so steep;
Li'l' girl she go fast asleep."

Every night the red-haired child
Begs to hear the story,
When the pasture ridges burn
With the sunset glory.

She can never understand,
Since the tale ends gladly,
Why her mother, telling it,
Always smiles so sadly.

Wonderingly she looks away
Where her mother's gazing;
Only sees the drifting herd,
In the sunset grazing.

[53]

SPANISH JOHNNY

The old West, the old time,
 The old wind singing through
The red, red grass a thousand miles,
 And, Spanish Johnny, you!
He'd sit beside the water-ditch
 When all his herd was in,
And never mind a child, but sing
 To his mandolin.

The big stars, the blue night,
 The moon-enchanted plain:
The olive man who never spoke,
 But sang the songs of Spain.
His speech with men was wicked talk—
 To hear it was a sin;
But those were golden things he said
 To his mandolin.

The gold songs, the gold stars,
 The world so golden then:
And the hand so tender to a child
 Had killed so many men.
He died a hard death long ago
 Before the Road came in;
The night before he swung, he sang
 To his mandolin.

AUTUMN MELODY

In the autumn days, the days of parting,
    Days that in a golden silence fall,
When the air is quick with bird-wings starting,
    And the asters darken by the wall;

Strong and sweet the wine of heaven is flowing,
    Bees and sun and sleep and golden dyes;
Long forgot is budding-time and blowing,
    Sunk in honeyed sleep the garden lies.

Spring and storm and summer midnight madness
    Dream within the grape but never wake;
Bees and sun and sweetness,—oh, and sadness!
    Sun and sweet that reach the heart—and break.

Ah, the pain at heart forever starting,
    Ah, the cup untasted that we spilled
In the autumn days, the days of parting!
    Would our shades could drink it, and be stilled.

PRAIRIE SPRING

Evening and the flat land,
Rich and somber and always silent;
The miles of fresh-plowed soil,
Heavy and black, full of strength and harshness;
The growing wheat, the growing weeds,
The toiling horses, the tired men;
The long, empty roads,
Sullen fires of sunset, fading,
The eternal, unresponsive sky.
Against all this, Youth,
Flaming like the wild roses,
Singing like the larks over the plowed fields,
Flashing like a star out of the twilight;
Youth with its insupportable sweetness,
Its fierce necessity,
Its sharp desire;
Singing and singing,
Out of the lips of silence,
Out of the earthy dusk.

MACON PRAIRIE
(NEBRASKA)

She held me for a night against her bosom,
The aunt who died when I was yet a baby,
The girl who scarcely lived to be a woman.
Stricken, she left familiar earth behind her,
Mortally ill, she braved the boisterous ocean,
Dying, she crossed irrevocable rivers,
Hailed the blue Lakes, and saw them fade forever,
Hungry for distances;—her heart exulting
That God had made so many seas and countries
To break upon the eye and sweep behind her.
From one whose love was tempered by discretion,
From all the net of caution and convenience
She snatched her high heart for the great adventure,
Broke her bright bubble under far horizons,—
Among the skirmishers that teased the future,
Precursors of the grave slow-moving millions
Already destined to the Westward-faring.

They came, at last, to where the railway ended,
The strange troop captained by a dying woman;
The father, the old man of perfect silence,
The mother, unresisting, broken-hearted,
The gentle brother and his wife, both timid,
Not knowing why they left their native hamlet;
Going as in a dream, but ever going.

In all the glory of an Indian summer,
The lambent transmutations of October,
They started with the great ox-teams from Hastings
And trekked in a southwesterly direction,
Boring directly toward the fiery sunset.
Over the red grass prairies, shaggy-coated,
Without a goal the caravan proceeded;
Across the tablelands and rugged ridges,
Through the coarse grasses which the oxen breasted,
Blue-stem and bunch-grass, red as sea-marsh samphire.
Always the similar, soft undulations
Of the free-breathing earth in golden sunshine,
The hardy wind, and dun hawks flying over
Against the unstained firmament of heaven.

In the front wagon, under the white cover,
Stretched on her feather-bed and propped with pillows,
Never dismayed by the rude oxen's scrambling,
The jolt of the tied wheel or brake or hold-back,
She lay, the leader of the expedition;
And with her burning eyes she took possession
Of the red waste,—for hers, and theirs, forever.

A wagon-top, rocking in seas of grasses,
A camp-fire on a prairie chartless, trackless,
A red spark under the dark tent of heaven.
Surely, they said, by day she saw a vision,
Though her exhausted strength could not impart it,—
Her breathing hoarser than the tired cattle.

[58]

When cold, bright stars the sunburnt days succeeded,
She took me in her bed to sleep beside her,—
A sturdy bunch of life, born on the ocean.
Always she had the wagon cover lifted
Before her face. The sleepless hours till daybreak
She read the stars.

"Plenty of time for sleep," she said, "hereafter."

She pointed out the spot on Macon prairie,
Telling my father that she wished to lie there.
"And plant, one day, an apple orchard round me,
In memory of woman's first temptation,
And man's first cowardice."
That night, within her bosom,
I slept.　　　　　　Before the morning
I cried because the breast was cold behind me.

Now, when the sky blazes like blue enamel,
Brilliant and hard over the blond cornfields,
And through the autumn days our wind is blowing
Like the creative breath of God Almighty—
Then I rejoice that offended love demanded
Such wide retreat, and such self-restitution;
Forged an explorer's will in a frail woman,
Asked of her perfect faith and renunciation,
Hardships and perils, prophecy and vision,
The leadership of kin, and happy ending
On the red rolling land of Macon prairie.

STREET IN PACKINGTOWN
(CHICAGO)

In the gray dust before a frail gray shed,
By a board fence obscenely chalked in red,
A gray creek willow, left from country days,
Flickers pallid in the haze.

Beside the gutter of the unpaved street,
Tin cans and broken glass about his feet,
And a brown whisky bottle, singled out
For play from prosier crockery strewn about,
Twisting a shoestring noose, a Polack's brat
Joylessly torments a cat.

His dress, some sister's cast-off wear,
Is rolled to leave his stomach bare.
His arms and legs with scratches bleed;
He twists the cat and pays no heed.
He mauls her neither less nor more
Because her claws have raked him sore.
His eyes, faint-blue and moody, stare
From under a pale shock of hair.
Neither resentment nor surprise
Lights the desert of those eyes—
To hurt and to be hurt; he knows
All he will know on earth, or need to know.

But there, beneath his willow tree,
His tribal, tutelary tree,
The tortured cat across his knee,
With hate, perhaps, a threat, maybe,
Lithuania looks at me.

A SILVER CUP

In Venice,
Under the Rialto bridge, one summer morning,
In a mean shop I bought a silver goblet.
It was a place of poor and sordid barter,
A damp hole filled with rags and rusty kettles,
Fire-tongs and broken grates and mended bellows,
And common crockery, coarse in use and fashion.
Everything spoke the desperate needs of body,
The breaking up and sale of wretched shelters,
The frail continuance even of hunger.
Misery under all—and that so fleeting!
The fight to fill the pots and pans soon over,
And then this wretched litter left from living.

The goblet
Stood in a dusty window full of charcoal,
The only bright, the only gracious object.
Because my heart was full to overflowing,
Because my day to weep had not come near me,
Because the world was full of love, I bought it.
From all the wreckage there I took no warning;—
Those ugly things outlasting hearts and houses,
And all the life that men build into houses.
Out of the jaws of hunger toothed with iron,
Into the sun exultantly I bore it.
Then, in the brightness of the summer sunshine,
I saw the loops and flourishes of letters,
The scattered trace of some outworn inscription,—
Six lines or more, rubbed flat into the silver,

Dashes and strokes, like rain-marks in a snowdrift.
Was it a prize, perhaps, or gift of friendship?
Was its inscription hope, or recognition?
Not heeding still, I bade my oarsman quicken,
And once ashore, across the Square I hastened,
Precipitate through the idlers and the pigeons,
Behind the Clock Tower, to a cunning craftsman,
There to exhort and urge the deft engraver,
And crowd upon my cup another story;
A name and promise in my memory singing.

In Venice,
Under the Rialto bridge, I bought you.
Now you come back to me, such long years after,
Your promise never kept, your hope defeated,
Your legend now a thing for tears and laughter;—
Though both your names are names of living people,
Cut by the steady hand of that engraver
While I stood over him and urged his deftness.
He played the part; nor stopped to smile and tell me
That for such words his art was too enduring.
His living was to cut such stuff in silver!
And now I have you, what to do, I wonder?
The names, another smith can soon efface them,—
But leave, so beautifully cut, the legend.
Not from a poet's book, but from the living
Sad mouth of a young peasant boy, I took it;
Four words, which mean that life is sweet together.

[63]

In some dark junk-shop window I shall leave you,
Some place of poor effects from broken houses,
Where desperate women go to sell a saucepan
And frightened men to buy a baby's cradle.
Here, in New York, a city full of exiles,
Short marriages and early deaths and heart-breaks:
In some such window, with the blue glass vases,
The busts of Presidents in plaster, gilded,
Pawned watches, and the rings and chains and bracelets
Given for love and sold for utter anguish,
There I shall leave you, a sole gracious object.

And hope some blind, bright eye will one day spy you—
Some boy with too much love and empty pockets
May read with quickening pulse your brief inscription,
Cut in his mother-language, half forgotten,
Four words which mean that life is sweet together;
Rush in and count his coins upon the table,
(A cup his own as if his heart had made it!)
And bear you off to one who hopes as he does.
So, one day, may the wish, for you, be granted.
They will not know, these two, the names you cover;
Mine and another, razed by violence from you,
Nor his, worn down by time, the first possessor's—
Who had his story, which you never told me.

RECOGNITION

The old volcanic mountains
That slope up from the sea—
They dream and dream a thousand years
And watch what-is-to-be.

What gladness shines upon them
When, white as white sea-foam,
To the old, old ports of Beauty
A new sail comes home!

GOING HOME
(BURLINGTON ROUTE)

How smoothly the trains run beyond the Missouri;
Even in my sleep I know when I have crossed the river.
The wheels turn as if they were glad to go;
The sharp curves and windings left behind,
The roadway wide open,
(*The crooked straight*
And the rough places plain.)

They run smoothly, they run softly, too.
There is not noise enough to trouble the lightest sleeper.
Nor jolting to wake the weary-hearted.
I open my window and let the air blow in,
The air of morning,
That smells of grass and earth—
Earth, the grain-giver.

How smoothly the trains run beyond the Missouri;
Even in my sleep I know when I have crossed the river.
The wheels turn as if they were glad to go;
They run like running water,
Like Youth, running away . . .
They spin bright along the bright rails,
Singing and humming,
Singing and humming.
They run remembering,
They run rejoicing,
As if they, too, were going home.

POOR MARTY

A lament for Martha, the old kitchenmaid, by her fellow servant, the stableman. The servants are not Negroes, but 'poor whites.'
(*Old Virginia*)

I

Who will scour the pots and pans,
Now Marty's gone away?
Who will scald the milking cans
And put the cream away?
Who will wash the goblets tall,
And chiney plates along the wall,
Platters big and platters small,
Never let one crack or fall,
Now Marty's gone away?
Ding-dong-dell, ding-dong-dell, poor Marty's gone away.

Who will clean the kitchen sink,
Ringed with grease as black as ink?
Not the Mistress, strict and cold,
Not the Master, meek and old,
Not our Miss in lawn and lace,
White of hand and fair of face.
Nor her sister, Marty's dear,
Played the harp for her to hear.
(Ever would the poor soul smile,
Rocking on her tired feet
When the harp strings sounded sweet—
Wiping all her goblets clear
To the music of her dear.)
Who will wash the things away,

Wash them three times every day?
Sixty years she never missed
While her hand hung to her wrist,
Never broke a plate or cup.
Who will wash our dishes up,
Now Marty's gone away?
Ding-dong-dell, ding-dong-dell, poor Marty's gone away.

Who will start the kitchen fire,
Now Marty's gone away?
When the house is all but dead,
Maids and mistress fast abed,
Windows rattle, stair steps groan,
Cookstove gray and cold as stone,
And the handle of the door
Froze to make your fingers sore.
Marty she was thin and old,
Little fleshed against the cold.
But she loved the maidies well,
Ever feared abroad to dwell.
All her life she feared to fall
Unto strangers after all,
To abide the poorhouse end.
Love and fear can both befriend.

Who will feed the winter birds,
Now Marty's gone away?
Snowbirds brown and robins red
Used to flutter round her head,

[68]

At the window open wide.
'T was our Mistress' fantasy
Neither cat nor dog might bide
For poor Marty's company,
But the birds came through the air
For the crust she had to spare.
Ding-dong-dell, ding-dong-dell, poor Marty's laid away.

II

On a moonlit winter night
Marty made her kitchen bright,
Wiped the pot-black from her hand
For before her Lord to stand,
She knew no other way.
No man earthly saw her go,
But she was gone afar we know
Before the break of day.
Mistress rang her silver bell,
Fixed to scold poor Marty well;
Master drummed his pewter pot
For his shaving water hot;
Miss and Missy waited long
Never thinking aught was wrong.
I must give my beasts their corn
With no bite or sup that morn,
For Marty's gone away.

Little had she here to leave,
Naught to will and none to grieve.

[69]

Hire nor wages did she draw
But her keep and bed of straw.
'T was our Mistress' fantasy
Marty might not trusted be
With fire to warm nor light to see,
In her kitchen loft.
But our Mistress could not bar
Light from moon or light from star,
Or from farther off.

'Martha,' said the angel, 'rise;
Come with me to Paradise.
Never heed thy needy shift,
Hers the shame who gave the gift.
Never hide thy choppy hand;
He, who waits, will understand
When He sees thee. Martha, rise;
Come with me to Paradise.'

Would that I prepared might be,
Clean of all this world like she;
Hands that never gathered aught,
But in faithful service wrought.
Naked as a babe new born
Went she forth that winter morn,
And not a stain she bare.
She, I pray, may housèd be
With Kindness, Love, and Charity—
Better off in ease than we,
Now poor Marty's gone.

[70]

A NOTE ON THE TYPE IN
WHICH THIS BOOK IS SET

This book is composed on the linotype in Bodoni, so called after its designer, Giambattista Bodoni (1740–1813) a celebrated Italian scholar and printer. Bodoni planned his type especially for use on the more smoothly finished papers that came into vogue late in the eighteenth century and drew his letters with a mechanical regularity that is readily apparent on comparison with the less formal old style. Other characteristics that will be noted are the square serifs without fillet and the marked contrast between the light and heavy strokes.

SET UP BY VAIL-BALLOU PRESS,
BINGHAMTON, N. Y. · PRINTED
AND BOUND BY THE PLIMPTON
PRESS, NORWOOD, MASS.
PAPER MADE BY S. D.
WARREN CO.,
BOSTON